SUPER BOWL SUPERSTARS

KURT WARNER
and the
St. Louis Rams

SUPER BOWL XXXIV

by Michael Sandler

Consultant: Norries Wilson
Head Football Coach
Columbia University

BEARPORT
PUBLISHING

NEW YORK, NEW YORK

Credits

Cover and Title Page, © Jeff Haynes/AFP/Getty Images; 4, © Tom Hauck/Getty Images; 5, © Jeff Haynes/AFP/Getty Images; 6, ©1988 The Gazette, Cedar Rapids, Iowa; 7, ©1989 The Gazette, Cedar Rapids, Iowa; 8, © Northern Iowa/Collegiate Images/Getty Images; 9, Courtesy of the University of Northern Iowa; 10, © AP Images/Eric Drotter; 11, Courtesy Jim Foster; 12, © Wayne Paulo/waynepaulo.com; 13, © Jonathan Daniel/Allsport/Getty Images; 14, © AP Images/Harold Jenkins; 15, © AP Images/James A. Finley; 16, © AP Images/Tim Nordmann; 17, © REUTERS/Tami Chappell; 18, © Don Emmert/AFP/Getty Images; 19, © Roberto Schmidt/AFP/Getty Images; 20, © Timothy A. Clary/AFP/Getty Images; 21, © Tony Ranze/AFP/Getty Images; 22L, © Tony Ranze/AFP/Getty Images; 22R, © AP Images/James A. Finley; 22 Background, © AP Images/John Bazemore.

Publisher: Kenn Goin
Senior Editor: Lisa Wiseman
Creative Director: Spencer Brinker
Design: Deborah Kaiser
Photo Researcher: Jennifer Bright

Library of Congress Cataloging-in-Publication Data

Sandler, Michael.
 Kurt Warner and the St. Louis Rams : Super Bowl XXXIV / by Michael Sandler.
      p. cm. — (Super Bowl superstars)
 Includes bibliographical references and index.
 ISBN-13: 978-1-59716-539-6 (library binding)
 ISBN-10: 1-59716-539-5 (library binding)
 1. Warner, Kurt, 1971–2. Football players—United States—Biography—Juvenile literature. 3. St. Louis Rams (Football team)—Juvenile literature. 4. Super Bowl (34th : 2000 : Atlanta, Ga.)—Juvenile literature. I. Title.

 GV939.W36S26 2008
 796.332092—dc22
 (B)
                                    2007009749

For more information, write to Bearport Publishing Company, Inc., 101 Fifth Avenue, Suite 6R, New York, New York 10003. Printed in the United States of America.

10 9 8 7 6 5 4 3 2 1

★ Contents ★

Super Bowl Dreams

With two minutes left in Super Bowl XXXIV (34), St. Louis Rams fans squirmed in their seats. The team had blown a 16-point lead. Would the Tennessee Titans steal their dreams of a Super Bowl title?

On the field, though, the Rams' quarterback Kurt Warner wasn't worried. He'd come too far to let this chance slip away. Kurt calmly dropped back in the **pocket** and let the ball fly.

In 2000, the St. Louis Rams (left) played the Tennessee Titans (right) in Super Bowl XXXIV (34).

Kurt Warner gets ready to pass the ball.

The St. Louis Rams had never won a Super Bowl.

Playing Quarterback

Kurt's football dream began in Iowa. There, as a child, he grew to love the game. Big, strong, and athletic, he was built for the sport.

When Kurt tried out for the high school team, he hoped to play **tight end**. After seeing Kurt throw the ball once, the coach had another idea. This kid was going to play quarterback.

Kurt (#13) played football for Regis High School in Cedar Rapids, Iowa.

Kurt (#43) shoots the ball during a high school basketball game.

Kurt didn't play only football in high school. He was also a star in basketball and baseball.

Unnoticed

Kurt became one of Iowa's best high school passers. Despite his skills, he wasn't **recruited** by many colleges to play on their football teams. Without **scholarship** offers, he went to a small school—the University of Northern Iowa.

Playing for a small school can make it hard to get noticed by National Football League (NFL) teams. When Kurt graduated, he wasn't **drafted** by a professional team.

Kurt dreamed of playing in the NFL. How could he get there?

Kurt played quarterback for the University of Northern Iowa.

Without an NFL team to play for, Kurt went to work in a supermarket.

While at the University of Northern Iowa, Kurt (#13) was named Gateway Conference Player of the Year (1993).

Arena Football

In 1994, Kurt found a way to keep playing football. He joined the Iowa Barnstormers. The Barnstormers weren't part of the NFL. This team played arena football.

The arena game is different from the NFL sport. It's played indoors on a tiny field. The action is faster and even more furious.

Kurt became the league's best quarterback. However, he wasn't satisfied. He longed for the phone to ring with an offer from an NFL team.

TAKIN

JOHN GRE
1996 LEAGU
COACH OF 1

Kurt (#13) playing for the Iowa Barnstormers

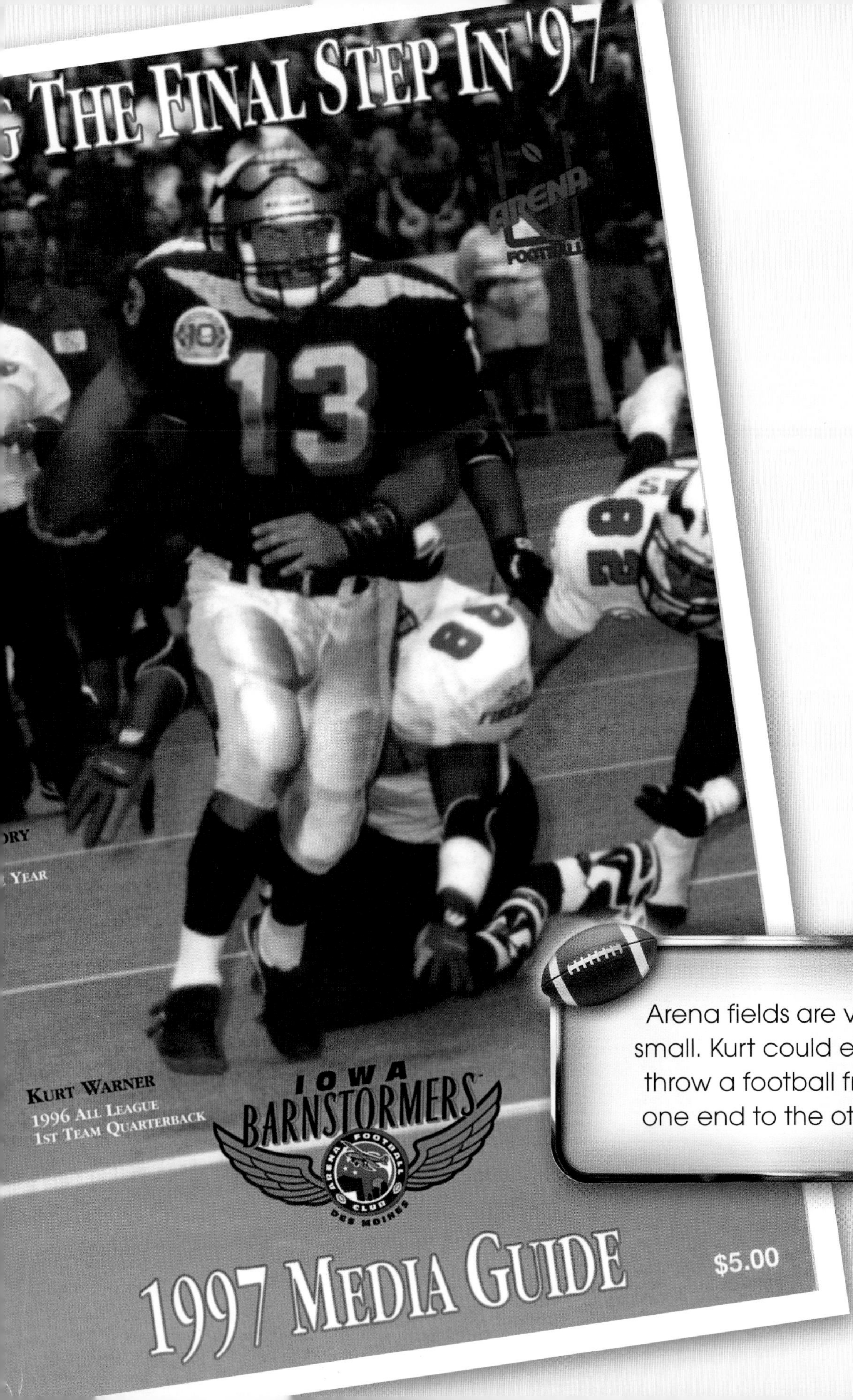

G THE FINAL STEP IN '97
ARENA
FOOTBALL
ORY
YEAR
KURT WARNER
1996 ALL LEAGUE
1ST TEAM QUARTERBACK
IOWA
BARNSTORMERS
ARENA FOOTBALL CLUB
DES MOINES
1997 MEDIA GUIDE
$5.00

Arena fields are very small. Kurt could easily throw a football from one end to the other.

Playing in Europe

Instead Kurt got a call from NFL Europe. This league was created by the NFL to help young players gain experience in the game. Teams play in European cities such as London and Frankfurt.

Kurt got a contract and a promise. If he played well, the NFL's St. Louis Rams would consider him for their team.

Kurt did his part. He led the Amsterdam Admirals to a first place finish. At season's end, he headed for the Rams' **training camp**.

Kurt calls a play to his teammates on the Amsterdam Admirals.

In 1998, Kurt (#10) finally got to wear an NFL uniform.

Kurt led NFL Europe in almost every passing category.

Getting a Chance

The St. Louis coaches didn't expect big things from Kurt. He barely made the team. For most of 1998, Kurt watched the action from the **sideline** as a **backup**.

Then, during the 1999 preseason, the Rams' **starting** quarterback got injured. Head coach Dick Vermeil needed a new starter. Suddenly Kurt's big chance had arrived.

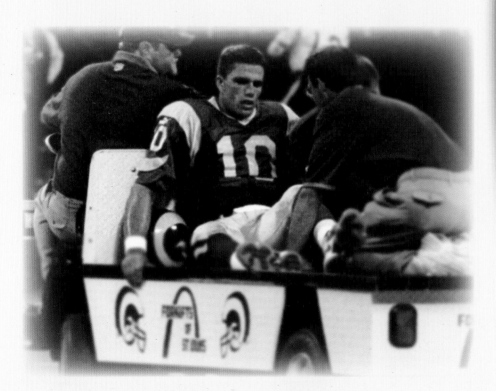

Trent Green was supposed to be the starting quarterback for the Rams.

Kurt during a practice

Kurt played in only
one game in 1998. He
threw just 11 passes.

Mystery Man

Few NFL players had heard of the Rams' new quarterback. However, they quickly learned his name. He didn't look like a beginner. He threw like a Hall of Fame passer.

Along with **Pro Bowl** running back Marshall Faulk, Kurt led the team to 13 wins and a trip to the playoffs. Then, with big wins against the Minnesota Vikings and the Tampa Bay Buccaneers, St. Louis moved into Super Bowl XXXIV (34).

Kurt is congratulated by fans after his first NFL start.

Marshall Faulk in action

In 1999, Kurt threw 41 touchdown passes. That season, he was named the NFL's Most Valuable Player (MVP).

Super Bowl XXXIV (34)

In Super Bowl XXXIV (34), the Rams faced the Tennessee Titans. Tennessee had been one of only three teams to beat St. Louis during the season. Winning wouldn't be easy.

The Titans had a great quarterback, Steve McNair. Their defense was tough as well. Jevon "the Freak" Kearse was a lightning-fast **pass rusher**. He had scared **opposing** quarterbacks all season long.

Early on in the game, Kurt threw the ball well. St. Louis slowly built a 16-0 lead.

Steve McNair (#9) is one of the few NFL quarterbacks who can run as well as throw.

Torry Holt (#88) celebrates a touchdown for St. Louis.

Kurt passed for
277 yards (253 m) in the
first half alone.

Roar of the Rams

Steve McNair, however, was too good not to fight back. Tennessee made three quick scores. With two minutes left, the game was tied.

Could Kurt save the game for St. Louis? He dropped back to throw. As he did, Jevon charged at him. Kurt was able to release the ball just before he was hit.

Isaac Bruce caught his pass for a St. Louis touchdown. The Rams won, 23-16. Kurt, the one-time arena quarterback, was now a Super Bowl champion!

Isaac Bruce (#80) runs for the winning touchdown for the Rams.

Kurt threw for 414 yards (379 m), breaking Joe Montana's Super Bowl record. He was named the MVP of the game.

★ Key Players ★

There were other key players on the St. Louis Rams who helped win Super Bowl XXXIV (34). Here are two of them.

★ Torry Holt #88

Position: Wide Receiver

Born: 6/5/1976 in Gibsonville, North Carolina

Height: 6' 0" (1.83 m)

Weight: 190 pounds (86 kg)

Key Plays: Caught seven passes including the Rams' first touchdown

★ Isaac Bruce #80

Position: Wide Receiver

Born: 11/10/1972 in Ft. Lauderdale, Florida

Height: 6' 0" (1.83 m)

Weight: 188 pounds (85 kg)

Key Play: Caught the winning touchdown pass with 1:54 left in the game

★ Glossary ★

backup (BAK-uhp)
a player who doesn't play at the start of a game

drafted (DRAFT-id)
picked to play for an NFL team after college

opposing (uh-POHZ-ing)
playing for the other team

pass rusher (PASS RUHSH-ur)
a defensive player who tries to tackle the quarterback before the quarterback throws the ball

pocket (POK-it)
the area on the field from where a quarterback throws the ball

Pro Bowl (PROH BOHL)
the yearly all-star game for the season's best NFL players

recruited (ri-KROOT-id)
asked to join

scholarship (SKOL-ur-ship)
an award that pays for a person to go to college

sideline (SIDE-line)
an area where players stand during games when they are not on the field

starting (START-ing)
playing at the start of a game; the best player at a position

tight end (TITE END)
an offensive player who catches passes and blocks for other players

training camp (TRAYNE-ing KAMP)
the place where NFL players practice before the season begins

Bibliography

Warner, Kurt. *All Things Possible: My Story of Faith, Football, and the Miracle Season.* San Francisco: HarperSanFrancisco (2000).

Wolfe, Rich. *Kurt Warner: And the Last Shall Be First.* Chicago: Triumph Books (2002).

St. Louis Post-Dispatch

Read More

Frisch, Aaron. *St. Louis Rams: Super Bowl Champions.* Mankato, MN: Creative Education (2005).

Rekela, George R. *Kurt Warner.* Berkeley Heights, NJ: Enslow (2003).

Schaefer, A. R. *Kurt Warner.* Mankato, MN: Capstone (2002).

Learn More Online

To learn more about Kurt Warner, the St. Louis Rams, and the Super Bowl, visit **www.bearportpublishing.com/SuperBowlSuperstars**

Index